Don't Lose Track *of* Time

Month by Month Planner

I0187388

Activinotes

Activinotes

DAILY JOURNALS, PLANNERS, NOTEBOOKS AND OTHER BLANK BOOKS

Monthly Planner

Monthly Planner

Monthly Planner

Monthly Planner

MONDAY	TUESDAY	WEDNESDAY	To Do List

Afternoon Schedules

Things to buy			

Monthly Planner

To Do List	THURSDAY	FRIDAY	SATURDAY

SUNDAY	NOTES

Things to buy		

Monthly Planner

MONDAY	TUESDAY	WEDNESDAY	To Do List

Afternoon Schedules

Things to buy			

Monthly Planner

To Do List	THURSDAY	FRIDAY	SATURDAY

Afternoon Schedules

SUNDAY			NOTES

Things to buy		

Monthly Planner

MONDAY	TUESDAY	WEDNESDAY	To Do List

Afternoon Schedules

Things to buy			

Monthly Planner

To Do List	THURSDAY	FRIDAY	SATURDAY

Afternoon Schedules

SUNDAY			NOTES

Things to buy		

Monthly Planner

MONDAY	TUESDAY	WEDNESDAY	To Do List

Afternoon Schedules

Things to buy			

Monthly Planner

To Do List	THURSDAY	FRIDAY	SATURDAY

Afternoon Schedules

SUNDAY		NOTES

Things to buy		

Monthly Planner

MONDAY	TUESDAY	WEDNESDAY	To Do List

Afternoon Schedules

Things to buy		

Monthly Planner

To Do List	THURSDAY	FRIDAY	SATURDAY

Afternoon Schedules

SUNDAY	NOTES

Things to buy		

Monthly Planner

MONDAY	TUESDAY	WEDNESDAY	To Do List

Afternoon Schedules

Things to buy		

Monthly Planner

To Do List	THURSDAY	FRIDAY	SATURDAY

Afternoon Schedules

SUNDAY	NOTES

Things to buy		

Monthly Planner

MONDAY	TUESDAY	WEDNESDAY	To Do List

Afternoon Schedules

Things to buy			

Monthly Planner

To Do List	THURSDAY	FRIDAY	SATURDAY

Afternoon Schedules

SUNDAY	NOTES

Things to buy		

Monthly Planner

MONDAY	TUESDAY	WEDNESDAY	To Do List

Afternoon Schedules

Things to buy			

Monthly Planner

To Do List	THURSDAY	FRIDAY	SATURDAY

Afternoon Schedules

SUNDAY	NOTES

Things to buy		

Monthly Planner

1
March

MONDAY	TUESDAY	WEDNESDAY	To Do List

Afternoon Schedules

Things to buy			

Monthly Planner

To Do List	THURSDAY	FRIDAY	SATURDAY

Afternoon Schedules

SUNDAY		NOTES

Things to buy		

Monthly Planner

MONDAY	TUESDAY	WEDNESDAY	To Do List

Afternoon Schedules

Things to buy			

Monthly Planner

To Do List	THURSDAY	FRIDAY	SATURDAY

SUNDAY	NOTES

Things to buy		

Monthly Planner

MONDAY	TUESDAY	WEDNESDAY	To Do List

Afternoon Schedules

Things to buy			

Monthly Planner

To Do List	THURSDAY	FRIDAY	SATURDAY

Afternoon Schedules

SUNDAY			NOTES

Things to buy		

Monthly Planner

MONDAY	TUESDAY	WEDNESDAY	To Do List

Afternoon Schedules

Things to buy			

Monthly Planner

To Do List	THURSDAY	FRIDAY	SATURDAY

Afternoon Schedules

SUNDAY		NOTES

Things to buy		

Monthly Planner

MONDAY	TUESDAY	WEDNESDAY	To Do List

Afternoon Schedules

Things to buy		

Monthly Planner

To Do List	THURSDAY	FRIDAY	SATURDAY

Afternoon Schedules

SUNDAY	NOTES

Things to buy		

Monthly Planner

MONDAY	TUESDAY	WEDNESDAY	To Do List

Afternoon Schedules

Things to buy			

Monthly Planner

To Do List	THURSDAY	FRIDAY	SATURDAY

Afternoon Schedules

SUNDAY		NOTES

Things to buy		

Monthly Planner

MONDAY	TUESDAY	WEDNESDAY	To Do List

Afternoon Schedules

Things to buy			

Monthly Planner

To Do List	THURSDAY	FRIDAY	SATURDAY

Afternoon Schedules

SUNDAY	NOTES

Things to buy		

Monthly Planner

MONDAY	TUESDAY	WEDNESDAY	To Do List

Afternoon Schedules

Things to buy			

Monthly Planner

To Do List	THURSDAY	FRIDAY	SATURDAY

Afternoon Schedules

SUNDAY		NOTES

Things to buy		

Monthly Planner

1 May

MONDAY	TUESDAY	WEDNESDAY	To Do List

Afternoon Schedules

Things to buy			

Monthly Planner

To Do List	THURSDAY	FRIDAY	SATURDAY

Afternoon Schedules

SUNDAY		NOTES

Things to buy		

Monthly Planner

MONDAY	TUESDAY	WEDNESDAY	To Do List

Afternoon Schedules

Things to buy			

Monthly Planner

To Do List	THURSDAY	FRIDAY	SATURDAY

Afternoon Schedules

SUNDAY	NOTES

Things to buy		

Monthly Planner

MONDAY	TUESDAY	WEDNESDAY	To Do List

Afternoon Schedules

Things to buy			

Monthly Planner

To Do List	THURSDAY	FRIDAY	SATURDAY

Afternoon Schedules

SUNDAY	NOTES

Things to buy		

Monthly Planner

MONDAY	TUESDAY	WEDNESDAY	To Do List

Afternoon Schedules

Things to buy			

Monthly Planner

To Do List	THURSDAY	FRIDAY	SATURDAY

Afternoon Schedules

SUNDAY	NOTES

Things to buy		

Monthly Planner

1
June

MONDAY	TUESDAY	WEDNESDAY	To Do List

Afternoon Schedules

Things to buy			

Monthly Planner

To Do List	THURSDAY	FRIDAY	SATURDAY

Afternoon Schedules

SUNDAY		NOTES

Things to buy		

Monthly Planner

MONDAY	TUESDAY	WEDNESDAY	To Do List

Afternoon Schedules

Things to buy		

Monthly Planner

To Do List	THURSDAY	FRIDAY	SATURDAY

Afternoon Schedules

SUNDAY		NOTES

Things to buy		

Monthly Planner

MONDAY	TUESDAY	WEDNESDAY	To Do List

Afternoon Schedules

Things to buy			

Monthly Planner

To Do List	THURSDAY	FRIDAY	SATURDAY

Afternoon Schedules

SUNDAY			NOTES

Things to buy		

Monthly Planner

MONDAY	TUESDAY	WEDNESDAY	To Do List

Afternoon Schedules

Things to buy			

Monthly Planner

To Do List	THURSDAY	FRIDAY	SATURDAY

Afternoon Schedules

SUNDAY	NOTES

Things to buy		

Monthly Planner

1
July

MONDAY	TUESDAY	WEDNESDAY	To Do List

Afternoon Schedules

Things to buy

Monthly Planner

To Do List	THURSDAY	FRIDAY	SATURDAY

Afternoon Schedules

SUNDAY		NOTES

Things to buy		

Monthly Planner

MONDAY	TUESDAY	WEDNESDAY	To Do List

Afternoon Schedules

Things to buy			

Monthly Planner

To Do List	THURSDAY	FRIDAY	SATURDAY

Afternoon Schedules

SUNDAY	NOTES

Things to buy		

Monthly Planner

MONDAY	TUESDAY	WEDNESDAY	To Do List

Afternoon Schedules

Things to buy			

Monthly Planner

To Do List	THURSDAY	FRIDAY	SATURDAY

SUNDAY	NOTES

Things to buy		

Monthly Planner

MONDAY	TUESDAY	WEDNESDAY	To Do List

Afternoon Schedules

Things to buy			

Monthly Planner

To Do List	THURSDAY	FRIDAY	SATURDAY

Afternoon Schedules

SUNDAY		NOTES

Things to buy		

Monthly Planner

1 August

MONDAY	TUESDAY	WEDNESDAY	To Do List

Afternoon Schedules

Things to buy			

Monthly Planner

To Do List	THURSDAY	FRIDAY	SATURDAY

Afternoon Schedules

SUNDAY			NOTES

Things to buy		

Monthly Planner

MONDAY	TUESDAY	WEDNESDAY	To Do List

Afternoon Schedules

Things to buy			

Monthly Planner

To Do List	THURSDAY	FRIDAY	SATURDAY

Afternoon Schedules

SUNDAY			NOTES

Things to buy		

Monthly Planner

MONDAY	TUESDAY	WEDNESDAY	To Do List

Afternoon Schedules

Things to buy			

Monthly Planner

To Do List	THURSDAY	FRIDAY	SATURDAY

Afternoon Schedules

SUNDAY			NOTES

Things to buy		

Monthly Planner

MONDAY	TUESDAY	WEDNESDAY	To Do List

Afternoon Schedules

Things to buy			

Monthly Planner

To Do List	THURSDAY	FRIDAY	SATURDAY

Afternoon Schedules

SUNDAY	NOTES

Things to buy		

Monthly Planner

MONDAY	TUESDAY	WEDNESDAY	To Do List

Afternoon Schedules

Things to buy		

Monthly Planner

To Do List	THURSDAY	FRIDAY	SATURDAY

Afternoon Schedules

SUNDAY	NOTES

Things to buy		

Monthly Planner

MONDAY	TUESDAY	WEDNESDAY	To Do List

Afternoon Schedules

Things to buy			

Monthly Planner

To Do List	THURSDAY	FRIDAY	SATURDAY

Afternoon Schedules

SUNDAY	NOTES

Things to buy		

Monthly Planner

MONDAY	TUESDAY	WEDNESDAY	To Do List

Afternoon Schedules

Things to buy			

Monthly Planner

To Do List	THURSDAY	FRIDAY	SATURDAY

Afternoon Schedules

SUNDAY	NOTES

Things to buy		

Monthly Planner

MONDAY	TUESDAY	WEDNESDAY	To Do List

Afternoon Schedules

Things to buy			

Monthly Planner

To Do List	THURSDAY	FRIDAY	SATURDAY

Afternoon Schedules

SUNDAY		NOTES

Things to buy		

Monthly Planner

MONDAY	TUESDAY	WEDNESDAY	To Do List

Afternoon Schedules

Things to buy			

Monthly Planner

To Do List	THURSDAY	FRIDAY	SATURDAY

Afternoon Schedules

SUNDAY	NOTES

Things to buy		

Monthly Planner

MONDAY	TUESDAY	WEDNESDAY	To Do List

Afternoon Schedules

Things to buy			

Monthly Planner

To Do List	THURSDAY	FRIDAY	SATURDAY

Afternoon Schedules

SUNDAY	NOTES

Things to buy		

Monthly Planner

MONDAY	TUESDAY	WEDNESDAY	To Do List

Afternoon Schedules

Things to buy			

Monthly Planner

To Do List	THURSDAY	FRIDAY	SATURDAY

Afternoon Schedules

SUNDAY			NOTES

Things to buy		

Monthly Planner

MONDAY	TUESDAY	WEDNESDAY	To Do List

Afternoon Schedules

Things to buy			

Monthly Planner

To Do List	THURSDAY	FRIDAY	SATURDAY

Afternoon Schedules

SUNDAY		NOTES

Things to buy		

Monthly Planner

1 November

MONDAY	TUESDAY	WEDNESDAY	To Do List

Afternoon Schedules

Things to buy			

Monthly Planner

To Do List	THURSDAY	FRIDAY	SATURDAY

Afternoon Schedules

SUNDAY			NOTES

Things to buy		

Monthly Planner

MONDAY	TUESDAY	WEDNESDAY	To Do List

Afternoon Schedules

Things to buy		

Monthly Planner

To Do List	THURSDAY	FRIDAY	SATURDAY

SUNDAY	NOTES

Things to buy		

Monthly Planner

MONDAY	TUESDAY	WEDNESDAY	To Do List

Afternoon Schedules

Things to buy		

Monthly Planner

To Do List	THURSDAY	FRIDAY	SATURDAY

Afternoon Schedules

SUNDAY			NOTES

Things to buy		

Monthly Planner

MONDAY	TUESDAY	WEDNESDAY	To Do List

Afternoon Schedules

Things to buy			

Monthly Planner

To Do List	THURSDAY	FRIDAY	SATURDAY

Afternoon Schedules

SUNDAY	NOTES

Things to buy		

Monthly Planner

1 December

MONDAY	TUESDAY	WEDNESDAY	To Do List

Afternoon Schedules

Things to buy			

Monthly Planner

To Do List	THURSDAY	FRIDAY	SATURDAY

Afternoon Schedules

SUNDAY	NOTES

Things to buy		

Monthly Planner

MONDAY	TUESDAY	WEDNESDAY	To Do List

Afternoon Schedules

Things to buy		

Monthly Planner

To Do List	THURSDAY	FRIDAY	SATURDAY

Afternoon Schedules

SUNDAY	NOTES

Things to buy		

Monthly Planner

MONDAY	TUESDAY	WEDNESDAY	To Do List

Afternoon Schedules

Things to buy			

Monthly Planner

To Do List	THURSDAY	FRIDAY	SATURDAY

Afternoon Schedules

SUNDAY			NOTES

Things to buy		

Monthly Planner

MONDAY	TUESDAY	WEDNESDAY	To Do List

Afternoon Schedules

Things to buy			

Monthly Planner

To Do List	THURSDAY	FRIDAY	SATURDAY

Afternoon Schedules

SUNDAY	NOTES

Things to buy		

Monthly Planner

Monthly Planner

Monthly Planner

Monthly Planner